The Movement

God's endtime plan to finish the work

by
Dan Vis

All Scripture quotations are from the
King James Version of the Bible
Emphasis supplied unless otherwise indicated.

ISBN: 978-0-9821805-2-5

Published by FAST Missions
111 2nd Street
Kathryn, ND 58049

Additional copies of this book are available by
visiting us at WWW.FAST.ST

Dedication

This book is dedicated to Sixto, Scott, Steve, Nick, Drew, Joel, Satavia, Monica, and others, who helped prove a local church can truly become an effective training center.

Table of Contents

The Movement
Preface

Many years ago, I gave my life to a cause. Something I call: *The Movement.* It wasn't an easy decision. And I was rather resistant at first. But after months of careful and deliberate study, I came to the conclusion it was the exact movement predicted in Bible prophecy for these last days. And that there was not even another possible fulfillment. The evidence was compelling, overwhelming even. So I decided to go all in.

It was one of the best decisions I've ever made. In the decades since, I've seen the Lord work in miraculous ways, through that movement. He's opened countless doors to me for ministry around the world. And everywhere I've gone, I've had the privilege to meet amazing people. In all the circumstances of life, and all the phases of life, that movement has always been there for me. It has been a true family–dearer in some ways, than my own flesh and blood.

I have no regrets, and were I younger today, I would only want to move more quickly and serve more enthusiastically.

But through those years, I've noticed a disturbing trend. For whatever reason, people aren't talking about the amazing prophecies connected with this movement near as much. We don't teach it, or at least don't emphasize it quite like we used to. And I fear it is causing some massive problems.

Everywhere, it seems, people are questioning, or ignorant of that clear prophetic identification. And as a result, to quote chapter one: "Suspicion and doubt are leavening many congregations. Millions in tithes have been diverted. And thousands of former members have turned their influence against us." Just when we most need all hands on deck, to face the final crisis, thousands are jumping ship.

Somehow, it seems we've failed to pass this vital Bible teaching down convincingly. Whether it's out of a desire to not come across as arrogant or boastful, or more likely, just a general neglect of Bible study–I don't know. But regardless, it's high time to dust off the old prophecies and take another look. To explore once again the powerful biblical evidence that supports our understanding of the movement. To reaffirm our traditional prophetic identification. And maybe even take a fresh peek at what God has in store for the movement, going forward.

It's been a while since I've seen a good book on the topic. And it just seems the right time to try and add one more to the stack. May the Lord use it to revive the confidence of many in the Seventh-day Adventist church as the remnant of Bible prophecy. That it really is, *The Movement...*

The Final Movement
Chapter 1

In mount Zion and in Jerusalem shall be deliverance,
as the LORD hath said,
and in the remnant whom the LORD shall call.
Joel 2:32

Isaiah is an interesting book. Just as the Bible is made up of 66 smaller books, Isaiah is made up of 66 smaller chapters. And even more interesting: just like the Bible is divided into two main sections, with 39 books in the Old Testament, and 27 in the New Testament, Isaiah is also divided into two main parts. The first 39 chapters are largely historical and biographical. Then in the last 27 chapters, there's a dramatic shift, with the content becoming distinctly more messianic and prophetic, even downright glorious.

You can take things even further, if you want. The first chapter in Isaiah hints at Genesis, and the fall of man, when God says the children "I have nourished and brought up ... have rebelled against me" (Isaiah 1:2). And then the last chapter brings Revelation to mind when it talks about "the new heavens and the new earth" God is going to make (Isaiah 66:22). The chapter that corresponds to the first book of the New Testament, prophesies John the Baptist as "the voice of him that crieth in the wilderness" (Isaiah 40:3). And the chapter that corresponds to Acts predicts an outpouring of the Spirit: "I will pour my spirit upon thy seed, and my blessing upon thine offspring" (Isaiah 44:3).

I suspect you could find other parallels too, if you looked. Maybe it's all just coincidence, but you have to admit it's at least curious!

Well lately, I've been spending a lot of time studying those final 27 chapters in Isaiah, and in the process made a fascinating discovery. Time and time again, these verses talk about something that should be dear to the heart of every believer: they talk about a powerful endtime movement, here on planet Earth...

The Remnant

The Bible, of course, mentions this movement in other places too. Revelation tells us the enemy, in the last days, would be "wroth with the woman", and "make war with the remnant of her seed" (Revelation 12:17).

But that's hardly the only place the Bible mentions a remnant:

II Kings 19:30
And the remnant that is escaped of the house of Judah shall yet again take root downward, and bear fruit upward.

Ezra 9:8
And now for a little space grace hath been shewed from the LORD our God, to leave us a remnant to escape.

Ezekiel 6:8
Yet will I leave a remnant, that ye may have some
that shall escape the sword among the nations,
when ye shall be scattered through the countries.

Micah 5:7
And the remnant of Jacob shall be in the midst of
many people as a dew from the LORD.

Actually, there are dozens of verses talking about a remnant from among God's people. Many of these refer primarily to a literal small group of Jewish survivors after one invasion or another, but it shows a clear pattern: while God may allow disaster to come to His people, He always saves a remnant for Himself.

A Chosen People
The Bible also suggests that understanding the identity of this remnant is quite important—because it is through this remnant, that God will communicate His final offer of deliverance to the world:

Joel 2:32
And it shall come to pass, that whosoever
shall call on the name of the LORD shall
be delivered: for in mount Zion and in
Jerusalem shall be deliverance, as the
LORD hath said, and in the remnant whom
the LORD shall call.

For many years, Bible scholars have taught the Seventh-day Adventist church was this endtime remnant, because of how closely it corresponds to all the identifying prophetic marks. We've argued it was raised up by God, at a specific time and place, to give a specific prophetic warning to the world. And historically, it did exactly that: spreading the three angel's messages around the world, to every nation, and kindred, and tongue, and people.

In my mind, there is little doubt this identification is correct. And in the days to come we'll explore some of the relevant prophetic evidence.

But in recent years, I have become increasingly troubled. Why? From my perspective, at least, it seems this vital Bible truth is being emphasized less and less each year.

Part of the reason may be a genuine desire to avoid coming across as arrogant or boastful. But I think the bigger reason is simply that we are not studying our Bibles as carefully as we used to. And especially Bible prophecy. Were our eyes to be fully opened to God's incredible plan for this endtime movement, I'm confident we'd be shouting about it from the housetop, rather than hiding it under a bushel.

A Church in Crisis

Whatever the cause, that neglect is causing real problems. Everywhere, it seems, people are rising up with the exact opposite message: that the church is apostate, corrupt, and heretical. The real message from heaven, they claim, is that we need to come out of her, withdraw our support, and go somewhere else for fellowship and spiritual nurture.

And it's costing the church dearly. Suspicion and doubt are leavening many congregations. Millions in tithes have been diverted. And thousands of former members have turned their influence against us. Just when the church most needs all the strength it can muster, it's being pummeled from every direction.

I believe it is high time to revive our study of God's plan for His endtime people. To dig deep into those prophecies outlining our past history, and future destiny. To pull back the veil on the incredible story surrounding this extraordinary final movement.

It's time to get serious about knowing what the Bible really says.

A Message for Zion

Before closing this first chapter, I'd like to share just one verse I stumbled on to while reading through those closing chapters of Isaiah. As a memorizer, I'm always on the lookout for verses that highlight the importance of memorizing, and this verse practically leaped off the page at me. Here it is:

Isaiah 51:16
And I have put my words in thy mouth, and I have covered thee in the shadow of mine hand, that I may plant the heavens, and lay the foundations of the earth, and say unto Zion, Thou art my people.

Incredible isn't it? God has a special work for those with His Word in their mouth, especially if they are able to spend some extended time alone with Him, hidden in the shadow of His hand. That work involves planting the essence or spirit of heaven in this dark, dreary world. And it involves laying here on earth a solid foundation, rooted in the core principles of Scripture. And the ministry I'm involved with, FAST Missions, like many other ministries, has been attempting to do these two things for years.

But there's a third special work mentioned in this verse, isn't there? And it goes right to the heart of our topic for today: that work is to "say unto Zion, Thou art my people".

What a vitally important message!

If it were just one verse, I might not have thought too much about it. But it's not. Those last 27 chapters are filled with incredible promises for God's people. By my count, close to 100 verses in that one short stretch of Scripture outlining a glorious bright future for God's people. We'll come back to some of them later in this book.

Plus, it's sprinkled through countless other passages of Scripture too. Actually, it's one of the most talked about themes in the Bible. I like to think of it as the Bible's second most important prophecy.

Yes, it's a big story. And it's compelling. And inspiring. It needs to get out.

So for the next few chapters, join me on an exciting adventure as we seek to discover what God has planned for His endtime people, and how we can be part of that plan.

It's time, don't you think?

Back to the Bible
Chapter 2

Until the times of restitution of all things,
which God hath spoken by the mouth
of all his holy prophets since the world began.
Acts 3:21

Ready to start learning more about the movement? God's endtime plan for finishing the work? If so, you are in for a treat—because we have multiple lines of Bible prophecy to explore over these next few chapters. So much in fact, it's hard to know where to start!

But there's probably no better place to start than the words of Jesus. He actually laid out one of the clearest and most important prophecies about earth's final movement anywhere in the Bible. And it's powerful, because it reveals one of the primary reasons for its existence.

Scattered Sheep

You can find the verse I'm thinking of in John chapter 10, where Jesus describes Himself as the good shepherd, and His true followers as those sheep who know His voice. It is in this context that Jesus makes the following prophecy:

John 10:16
And other sheep I have, which are not of this fold:
them also I must bring, and they shall hear my
voice; and there shall be one fold, and one
shepherd.

It tells us a couple important things. First, that God's people have historically been divided into different groups. Second, that this was never God's purpose or desire. And perhaps most important, third, the day is coming when there will be just one fold at last.

Some time back, I remember reading an article somewhere that estimated there were approximately 30,000 Christian denominations. Groups all divided primarily by incompatible interpretations of Scripture. To make matters worse, this number surely fails to take into account the multitudes of independent congregations who follow whatever peculiar theological views their pastor happens to hold.

This is hardly the unity Jesus asked for in His great apostolic prayer, when He prayed for those "which shall believe on me" that "they all may be one" (John 17:20-21). And that's a problem.

Why? The prophecies of Jesus are certain. And His prayers are sure. In other words, we have every reason to expect to see some heaven-ordained movement in our day, gathering people into a single united faith.

A Restitution of All Things

Peter certainly believed it would happen. In his second recorded sermon in the book of Acts, Peter prophesied a special time of refreshing, just before the return of Christ (Acts 3:19-20). He then explained that Jesus would remain in heaven "until the times of restitution of all things, which God hath spoken by the mouth of all his holy prophets since the world began" (Acts 3:21). In other words, a restoration of basic Bible truth has to take place before Jesus can come back. Incredible.

And actually, the Bible warns there would be an urgent need for this endtime rediscovery of truth. Because error would be so rampant.

To overly simplify things, the history of the Christian church has been pretty confused almost from the start. The early church was riddled with factions ranging from Jewish legalism to Greek Gnosticism. Paul warned, "I know this, that after my departing shall grievous wolves enter in among you, not sparing the flock ... speaking perverse things, to draw away disciples after them" (Acts 20:29-30).

This accelerated all through the dark ages, until there was a widespread general apostasy from sound biblical teachings. The prophet Daniel spoke of the dominant religious power during this time, describing how "it cast down the truth to the ground, and it practised, and prospered" (Daniel 8:12).

During the reformation period, a number of commendable attempts were made to recover key Bible truths, but rather than their path being like a "shining light, that shineth more and more unto the perfect day" (Proverbs 4:18), all of these reform movements quickly stalled and ceased their forward progress. The Holy Spirit was willing to guide them "into all truth" (John 16:13), but none of these groups seemed ready to follow all the way.

In coming down to our day, we see the Bible predicts confusion about the Bible would be even more pervasive. And the fragmentation of Christianity into tens of thousands of denominations is clear proof error and deception has indeed multiplied, not diminished.

I Timothy 4:1
In the latter times some shall depart from the faith, giving heed to seducing spirits, and doctrines of devils.

II Timothy 3:13
But evil men and seducers shall wax worse and worse, deceiving, and being deceived.

II Timothy 4:3-4
For the time will come when they will not endure sound doctrine ... and they shall turn away their ears from the truth, and shall be turned unto fables.

The New Testament abounds with warnings about false teachers and their deceptive teachings. Clearly, with so many "winds of doctrine" blowing today (Ephesians 4:14), sorting out what is actually truth can be a treacherous task.

A Cause for Hope

But at the same time, there is cause for hope. According to Paul, the various gifts of apostle, prophet, evangelist, pastor, and teacher (Ephesians 4:11) were given "for the edifying of the body of Christ: till we all come in the unity of the faith, and of the knowledge of the Son of God" (Ephesians 4:12-13). In other words, God is going to keep working at it until He finally has a people able to uphold the core truths of the Bible, and share them with the world.

In particular:

- They will know the truth about the law of God, and the fourth commandment.
- They will know the truth about what happens after death. The truth about heaven. The truth about hell.
- They will know the truth about the manner of Christ's return and understand the basic sequence of endtime events.
- They will know about the temple in heaven, and the priestly ministry of Christ. They will understand basic Old Testament typology.
- They will know the truth about the Godhead. The full deity of Christ. The full personality of the Holy Spirit.
- They will know the truth about speaking in tongues. About evolution and creation. Predestination vs free will. The correct method of baptism. And all sorts of other topics that divide churches today.
- And of course, they will know the truth about sin, the sacrifice of Jesus, and the salvation available through faith in Him.

While I don't have time to address any of these points here, the fact is, on each given topic there is only one correct position. And whatever that whole bundle of correct positions looks like, God's plan is to tie it all together, and give it to one group, so the world can see the whole picture in context, at last. Only then can the world make a final informed decision about Christ.

An Exalted Mountain

The Old Testament actually predicts this exact thing.

That God will indeed raise up such a group, and through them, get the truth out to the world:

> *Micah 4:1-2*
> *But in the last days it shall come to pass, that the mountain of the house of the LORD shall be established in the top of the mountains, and it shall be exalted above the hills; and people shall flow unto it. And many nations shall come, and say, Come, and let us go up to the mountain of the LORD, and to the house of the God of Jacob; and he will teach us of his ways, and we will walk in his paths: for the law shall go forth of Zion, and the word of the LORD from Jerusalem.*

Now here's one reason I believe the Seventh-day Adventist church is that endtime "house of the Lord" from which "the word of the LORD" is going forth. And it's not just because I happen to agree with its theological position on all those points listed above. It has to do with how this whole movement came into being.

You see, virtually every one of those 30,000 denominations came about pretty much the same way. Some person saw something in Scripture that didn't seem to match what the leaders of their church taught—and when they confronted their church leaders they encountered resistance. So they broke off and started a new denomination, taking some portion of their old church membership with them. In other words, they split off, making only one or two small changes, in either a right or wrong direction, and pretty much kept everything else as it was.

But the Seventh-day Adventist church arose through a completely different process. Thousands of believers from every major denomination heard a compelling prophetic message, heralded by a diverse mixture of advent preachers. And then, after a painful disappointment sifted out those who were insincere or shallow in their commitment, they were finally led to organize a brand new denomination. From scratch.

Imagine the challenge of trying to unite all those representatives from so many different religious backgrounds into one shared faith! It forced them to reexamine each and every point of doctrine. Doctrinal positions were proposed, challenged, adjusted and fine-tuned, through much discussion, thoughtful consideration and agonizing prayer. It was terribly difficult, no doubt, but they persevered. And with the help of a little divine guidance, they eventually constructed an entirely new system of beliefs.

Nothing like it has ever happened in the history of the Christian church. Nor is it likely to ever happen again.

It took the voice of the Good Shepherd, calling to all His sheep wherever they happened to be. And gathering them together. Leading them through a difficult but necessary process into an extraordinary oneness of faith. One fold, one Shepherd.

The promised "restitution of all things" happened, miraculously, exactly as foretold. God raised up a bright light that has only continued to shine brighter and brighter, "more and more unto the perfect day". He has caused "the house of the Lord" to be "exalted", and through it, God is sending "the Word of the Lord" to all the world. And that message today, still draws people from all other faiths—because every one of its positions is tested and tried.

It's glorious, if you think about it. A global movement, to rediscover and proclaim all the foundational teachings of the Bible. A movement back to the Bible.

Don't you want to be part of it?

Enemies of the Gospel
Chapter 3

The god of this world hath blinded the minds
of them which believe not,
lest the light of the glorious gospel of Christ,
who is the image of God, should shine unto them.
II Corinthians 4:4

Welcome back to another exciting study in Bible prophecy. And in particular, another study into God's plan for His endtime movement. His plan to finish the work.

Over the next few chapters we're going to look at this vital topic from a number of different perspectives. Today, I want to look at it in terms of earth's final warning.

The Final Warning

You see, in addition to God wanting a movement that reveals the basic truths of the Bible correctly, He wants a movement that will give a specific warning to the world. An endtime, prophetic message.

That message, of course, is found in Revelation 14. There, God uses three angels to communicate important truths every person on planet earth needs to hear. Here is what those angels have to say:

Revelation 14:6-11
1) And I saw another angel fly in the midst of heaven, having the everlasting gospel to preach unto them that dwell on the earth, and to every nation, and kindred, and tongue, and people, Saying with a loud voice, Fear God, and give glory to him; for the hour of his judgment is come: and worship him that made heaven, and earth, and the sea, and the fountains of waters.
2) And there followed another angel, saying, Babylon is fallen, is fallen, that great city, because she made all nations drink of the wine of the wrath of her fornication.
3) And the third angel followed them, saying with a loud voice, If any man worship the beast and his image, and receive his mark in his forehead, or in his hand, The same shall drink of the wine of the wrath of God, which is poured out without mixture into the cup of his indignation...

There's a lot in these verses that we don't have time to unpack now: The fear of the Lord. What it means to give glory to God. The fact God's judgment has already commenced. The identity of spiritual Babylon. But for the moment, I just want to zoom in on the message of the third angel.

Here God is warning in the sternest language possible, that a great test is coming to every man, woman, and child. Each will be forced to choose whether they will receive the Mark of the Beast, or refuse it. And their eternal destiny hangs in the balance.

Those who refuse the Mark will be outlawed, forbidden to buy or sell, and ultimately sentenced to death. Those who give in to that pressure and receive the Mark, will drink the cup of God's wrath, unmingled with mercy. Serious stuff!

It's worth noting that some people have a strange desire to pick up some other issue and make that man's final testing truth. To do so is to miss the whole point of this passage. Don't fall for it. Man's ultimate challenge is specified right here: the Mark of the Beast.

Now the previous chapter in Revelation outlines the principle actors in this final showdown. The Antichrist, or leopard-like beast, is the originator of the Mark. And the False Prophet, a two-horned beast rising up out of the earth, is the one who compels the world to receive it. These two powers work together closely, to push the whole world into open rebellion against the law of God.

Now if you have never studied these prophecies, feel free to skip the next couple paragraphs and continue on to the next section where I get into what's so strange about this warning.

For the rest of you, here's a bit of quick review.

First, these beasts refer to very real, political states. The Antichrist beast represents the Roman Catholic system, which ruled the medieval world for well over a thousand years, received a deadly wound in 1798 with the dissolution of the Papal States, only to resurrect once again as a sovereign nation in 1929, with the establishment of Vatican City.

The False Prophet represents the United States of America, a late blooming, slow growing empire, that started out with lamblike horns, but has since come to speak like a dragon. It is this nation which dominates the world militarily, economically, and politically today.

The Mark represents a false day of worship, an emblem of the papacy's claim of authority to change the law of God. And

– 16 –

the USA will insist all observe this false day in a direct contradiction to its core constitutional principle of religious freedom. That conflict is fraught with profound theological implications that go far beyond the scope of today's study.

Truth is Stranger than Fiction

Now here's the point: Seventh-day Adventists have been preaching this message with great clarity for well over 170 years. But who else?

Given that this warning is to go to "every nation, and kindred, and tongue, and people", it seems strange that virtually no other group is really explaining these verses. It's even more odd when you consider how high the stakes really are.

These verses represent earth's most solemn warning. And our reception of this message seals our fate, one way or the other. Yet pretty much every other Christian group out there either ignores these verses, or twists their meaning into something completely unrecognizable. How could that be?

What makes this more bizarre still, is that virtually every Protestant denomination at one point knew the correct identity of the Antichrist. During the Reformation, every major reformer was crystal clear on it. Luther, Calvin, Zwingli, Huss, Tyndale, Knox, and countless others all wrote about it explicitly. The overwhelming prophetic evidence, they argued, pointed straight to the Church of Rome.

But in the counter-reformation, Catholic theologians began developing alternate interpretations of prophecy, such as futurism, which pushes the Antichrist off into the far future, and preterism, which limits the Antichrist to the distant past. These theories were invented by men in a brazen attempt to shift the prophetic spotlight away from their own organization.

But in what is certainly one of the most extraordinary twists of history, pretty much all of these "protest" denominations gradually came to adopt one or the other of these Catholic inventions, and the prophetic views of their founding leaders were relegated to the dust bin of history. The voice of the Reformation has been almost completely squelched.

The fact this could happen proves one thing for sure: truth really can be stranger than fiction!

The True Gospel

But God didn't raise up the Seventh-day Adventist church merely to expose the Antichrist system. Or to identify the False Prophet (first done by the Adventist theologian J. N. Andrews in 1851). Or even to point out the true significance of the Mark of the Beast in relation to worship. The real work of the church was to proclaim the everlasting gospel.

That's actually how the three angel's messages begin: "I saw another angel fly in the midst of heaven, having the everlasting gospel to preach unto them that dwell on the earth" (Revelation 14:6). That's the heart of the message. And the two accompanying angels are sent primarily to bring added clarity and focus to that message.

Or to put it differently, the Antichrist and False Prophet represent two distortions of the gospel.

The Antichrist system is essentially a system of salvation by works. The various sacraments of the Catholic church are all supposed to convey merit, which contributes to salvation. But the Bible is crystal clear: "by the deeds of the law there shall no flesh be justified in his sight" (Romans 3:20).

The Protestant churches of the False Prophet system tend to go to the other extreme. Belief alone, without any transformation in the life, is enough to secure eternal life. But the Bible is equally clear that this view is false too: "He that saith, I know him, and keepeth not his commandments, is a liar, and the truth is not in him" (I John 2:4).

What's needed is a gospel that avoids both ditches. It know that only the shed blood of Christ can atone for our sins. But also that saving faith taps into real power for obedience. While we are saved by faith alone, it is always a faith that works. For faith without works is dead. (James 2:20). The gospel lies at the intersection of both these truths.

It's a gospel neither the Antichrist nor False Prophet can give. In fact, no church can teach that gospel if it is drunk with the wine of Babylon. The true gospel requires a sober-minded system of basic theology. That's the point of the second angel.

Nor can a church teach this gospel if it is promoting a day of worship contrary to the law of God. The true gospel not only sees the sacrifice of Christ as an atonement for our violation of God's unchanging moral law, but also as a way to tap into power for obedience to that same law. That's the point of the third angel.

The gospel is like a golden coin. It has two sides to it, pardon and power—and there's no way to separate them.

A Global Issue

And that's the real strategy of the enemy, isn't it? It is not just to persecute people for going to church on a different day. Rather, he understands that the "gospel of Christ ... is the power of God unto salvation to every one that believeth" (Romans 1:16). And he's determined to do everything possible to rob believers of their salvation. So the enemy works hardest to undermine, corrupt, and distort the essence of the gospel.

On the other side, God is doing everything possible to raise up a final movement to proclaim the gospel clearly. A global, international organization committed to reaching an entire planet. Not some fringe group here or there, but a worldwide system capable of reaching every nation, kindred, tongue, and people. A movement raised up to give a lost and dying world one last chance to be saved.

There is only one global organization giving this everlasting gospel in the context of its prophetic warning. And it does span the world–with representatives in more countries than any other Protestant denomination. It's an incredible fulfillment of prophecy. One lone, global church, proclaiming the most solemn warning of Scripture. And no one else is giving it!

It's astonishing really. The only explanation is that it's a movement of God.

Order of Melchisedec
Chapter 4

And the place of the sanctuary was cast down.
And an host was given him against
the daily sacrifice by reason of transgression
Daniel 8:11-12

Hello again. And welcome back to another study in God's plan for His endtime people. His purpose for the movement. Today, in particular, I want to talk about the sanctuary.

It's an important subject. In fact, it was largely the rediscovery of this Bible truth that sparked the birth of the movement. It's also a critical key to understanding the book of Revelation, which is laced with sanctuary symbolism and typology. And much like the other topics we've explored these last few chapters, there is pretty much only one group in the world able to effectively teach this subject: the Seventh-day Adventist church.

But I'm getting ahead of myself. Let's back up a bit, and pick up the pieces one by one.

Lost and Found

In the book of Daniel we find several descriptions of the

Antichrist, that help contribute to its identification. In chapter 8, we have this important picture of the work of the Antichrist:

Daniel 8:10-12
And it waxed great, even to the host of heaven ... Yea, he magnified himself even to the prince of the host, and by him the daily sacrifice was taken away, and the place of the sanctuary was cast down. And an host was given him against the daily sacrifice by reason of transgression.

While there are varying views on exactly what these verses refer to, it seems clear to me the Roman Catholic system wanted to put itself in the place of Christ. As Paul wrote later, he "opposeth and exalteth himself above all that is called God, or that is worshipped; so that he as God sitteth in the temple of God, showing himself that he is God" (II Thessalonians 2:4). Rather than pointing people to the priestly ministry of Christ in heaven, he turned people's attention to its earthly services, its earthly priests, its earthly buildings. And vast multitudes were effectively led astray by this terrible "transgression". The place of the sanctuary was cast down.

Next in Daniel's vision, he hears two beings talking about what was done. One asks "how long shall be the vision concerning the daily sacrifice, and the transgression of desolation, to give both the sanctuary and the host to be trodden under foot"? The other answers, "unto two thousand and three hundred days; then shall the sanctuary be cleansed" (Daniel 8:13-14).

Apparently, the Antichrist's power to deceive people about the sanctuary in heaven would be broken at a specific point in time. And by implication, the truth would then be restored once again.

The early Advent preachers stumbled on to this time prophecy, and were able to successfully link it with the subsequent vision in Daniel chapter 9, and use that to calculate the time of it's fulfillment: 1844. They did not fully understand the event predicted, of course, because that would require the sanctuary truth to be restored prior to the appointed time. Instead, they assumed this cleansing of the sanctuary would be the return of Christ—to their eventual disappointment. But when the specified time did roll around, the truth unlocked right on schedule. An Advent preacher walking through a corn field suddenly realized the sanctuary in question must be the temple in heaven. And like dominos, all the pieces quickly fell into place.

Don't miss that point: the truth of the sanctuary was restored at the exact time predicted. And it was given to the exact movement God was raising up.

The Book of Hebrews

Seventh-day Adventists today kind of take this topic of the sanctuary for granted. For the most part, we all believe there is a literal temple in heaven. That Jesus is serving there as our high priest. That the Old Testament feasts, like the Passover and Day of Atonement, were typological, pointing to specific future fulfillments. And for a long time, we've known what really did happen in 1844.

But without the book of Hebrews, it might be a different story.

You see, outside that book (which I'm going to assume was written by Paul), there is not a single verse in the New Testament that refers to Jesus as our high priest. Or even as a priest!

I might have missed something, but when I typed "priest" in my computer, I didn't find much. The four gospels and Acts have a few references to the Jewish high priest, and various other earthly priests. And Revelation makes a couple references to believers being made priests. But apart from Hebrews, not a word about Jesus.

Fortunately, Hebrews does do an amazing job—laying out a complete theology of the sanctuary in heaven. Better still, God saw fit to get that book included in the canon of Scripture, and preserved it down to our day. God clearly wanted His endtime movement to understand this topic. And through them, to tell it to the world.

A New Order

Now Paul pretty much uses the whole book of Hebrews to make his point about the priestly ministry of Christ. And he builds his entire argument on one obscure, rather puzzling verse. A verse that references another obscure, rather puzzling event.

It's fascinating to watch his mind at work!

Here's the nutshell version of the book. Basically, Paul makes the claim Jesus is better. A better high priest. Serving in a better temple. Offering better sacrifices. And so on.

And he gives at least 8 proofs to support this claim all rooted in just one verse:

Psalms 110:4
The LORD hath sworn, and will not repent, Thou art a priest for ever after the order of Melchizedek.

Now, Paul is well justified in connecting this verse to Jesus. The whole context of this passage is clearly messianic. In fact, Jesus used the first verse of this chapter to silence the Pharisees giving Him trouble in the temple. And he connected it clearly to the "Christ" (See Psalms 110:1, Matthew 22:42-45).

So if this verse is talking about Jesus, we have good evidence here He is called to be a priest.

But Paul goes much farther in breaking down this verse, in what can only be considered a masterpiece of exegesis. Here is a quick summary of his points:

1) The earthly priesthood was established when Aaron was called by God to be high priest. In the same way, this verse makes clear, it is God himself that calls this new priesthood into existence. Hebrews 5:4-6.

2) This verse makes clear God will confirm this new priesthood with an oath, when it says "the LORD hath sworn". In the same way, God swore an oath to Abraham to establish the "immutability of His counsel". Hebrews 6:13-19.

3) Melchisedec is clearly a type of Christ. The fact we know neither his parentage nor his descendants foreshadows Jesus, who has "neither beginning of days, nor end of life". Furthermore, his name means king of righteousness, and his title, king of peace. Fitting descriptions of Jesus. Hebrews 7:2-3.

4) Melchisedec was greater than Abraham, evidenced by two incontrovertible facts. First Abraham was blessed by him, and second Abraham gave tithes to him. Hebrews 7:6-10. In the same way, Jesus is greater than any earthly priest.

5) The fact another priesthood is coming proves the Levitical system was transitory. Being of the tribe of Judah, rather than of Levi, Jesus is clearly a new kind of priest. And His is a priesthood that continues "forever". Hebrews 7:11-14.

6) The Levitical system was operated by a long succession of weak, mortal men, with no power to deliver anyone from sin. But the priesthood of Christ is unchanging, powered by an endless life. It's a priesthood that can save us to the uttermost. Hebrews 7:16-17, Hebrews 7:24-25.

7) If the earthly priesthood was just a type of a heavenly priesthood, then the earthly temple, which was modeled on a pattern shown to Moses in the mount, must be a type too. Or to put it differently, there must be a real temple, the original, in heaven—where Christ ministers for us. Hebrews 8:1-2, Hebrews 8:5.

8) And if that's true, then it just makes sense the whole system of ceremonies and rituals must be typological too. Not just the priests, and the temple, but the sacrifices, the feasts, and everything else. They are all prophecies set to dissipate when their fulfillment arrived. Hebrews 9:1-10

Paul is making a dramatic argument. That this one obscure verse in Psalms, alluding to one obscure incident in the life of Abraham, is the foundation for a whole series of arguments, demolishing the entire Jewish Levitical system and replacing it with a brand new order. The order of Melchisedec. Wow.

A New Covenant

Essentially, Paul is establishing the terms of a whole new covenant between God, and His people. A "better covenant" established upon "better promises" (Hebrews 8:6).

To adopt this new covenant, with it's new priesthood, temple, sacrifice, and systems—is to move from type to antitype. From shadow to substance. From a system that is transitory and powerless to one that is eternal, and life-changing. A system full of incredible possibilities!

Here is God's part in this new covenant:

Hebrews 10:16-17
This is the covenant that I will make with them after those days, saith the Lord, I will put my laws into their hearts, and in their minds will I write them; And their sins and iniquities will I remember no more.

Basically, God promises two things. First, to imprint the principles of His Law in our heart and mind. To transform our character into His likeness, in a way the old covenant never could. And second, that our sins would be forgotten. Blotted out. Cast into the depths of the sea.

Both are amazing good news!

For our part, we are to "draw near with a true heart in full assurance of faith" (Hebrews 10:22). "Hold fast the profession of our faith without wavering" (Hebrews 10:23). "Consider one another to provoke unto love and to good works" (Hebrews 10:24).

We must "cast not away" our "confidence" (Hebrews 10:35). We "have need of patience" that we "might receive the promise (Hebrews 10:36). We must "believe to the saving of the soul" (Hebrews 10:39). Ultimately, it boils down to this: "the just shall live by faith" (Hebrews 10:38).

God promises to work the miracle we need, both in how we live today, and in terms of the record of our past. Our part is to believe He does both.

The sanctuary is a beautiful message. It unlocks all sorts of mysteries. It shines a spotlight on numerous prophecies. And on God's plan for our salvation. It's a message that needs to get out to the world.

And only one one group in the world has this information. One church. One organization. One movement. And it started preaching about it, at the exact moment foretold!

The Promised Gift
Chapter 5

Even as the testimony of Christ was confirmed in you:
So that ye come behind in no gift;
waiting for the coming of our Lord Jesus Christ:
I Corinthians 1:6-7

So far, we've been exploring a number of different Bible themes that helps us to identify God's endtime movement. And even more, to understand its purpose. To paint a picture of why it is so important.

We looked at the need for a people who can give a clear and accurate, explanation of the basic truths of the Bible. A people able to proclaim the everlasting gospel, in its proper prophetic context. And a people able to grasp and share the priestly ministry of Christ, in all its New Testament glory.

We've also seen that only one movement matches any of these identifying marks. The Seventh-day Adventist church.

God clearly prophesied such a movement would arise, and historically it happened just as predicted.

But a question may be running through your mind. How did it all come about? How could one organization achieve so much clarity in terms of systematic theology, endtime prophecy, and sanctuary typology. That's an incredible amount of insight.

In today's study we look at part of the answer to that question. And it involves a vital gift.

A Short History Lesson

The book of Revelation, in chapter 12, gives a short but insightful history of the church. We don't have time to study it in detail here, but it's worth taking a few moments to hit the highlights.

In this chapter, God's church is described as a glorious, pure woman. And the enemy is described as a great red dragon seeking to destroy this woman. In the middle part of this chapter we see a great conflict take place between Christ and Satan, revolving around the cross. After Christ ascends to heaven, we see in verse 13, the defeated dragon turning his focus toward the woman.

The woman then flees into the wilderness for a time, times, and half a time, a prophetic period of 1260 years mentioned elsewhere in Daniel and Revelation, corresponding to an extended time of papal persecution. Bible scholars have identified that period as running from 538 to 1798. During these years, God's people had to largely live their lives in hiding.

Near the end of that period, the earth helps the woman, by opening her mouth, and swallowing a flood of people. Historically, the New World was discovered around this time, and waves of colonists emigrated to America—often in search of religious freedom. The true church jumped the Atlantic and took root in America.

Which brings us down to the final verse. The enemy's last assault against God's people. Against the remnant. Against the movement. Notice:

Revelation 12:17
And the dragon was wroth with the woman, and
went to make war with the remnant of her seed,
which keep the commandments of God, and have
the testimony of Jesus Christ.

Putting it all together we can glean a number of important details about the remnant. First, its origins would seem to be rooted in the New World. Second, it would arise after 1798, and the end of papal persecution. Third, it is identified as keeping the commandments of God—including the fourth, which involves observance of the true Sabbath. And last but not least, it has the testimony of Jesus.

It is this testimony of Jesus, that I want to zoom in on today.

The Testimony of Jesus

If you are familiar with this topic, you probably know the Bible speaks elsewhere about this testimony of Jesus. But you may not know just how deep this topic really goes.

The usual starting point is Revelation 19:10, which gives us an interesting synonym for it. Here John sees a glorious angel in vision, and falls at his feet to worship him. Notice carefully the angel's response:

Revelation 19:10
And I fell at his feet to worship him. And he said
unto me, See thou do it not: I am thy
fellowservant, and of thy brethren that have the
testimony of Jesus: worship God: for the
testimony of Jesus is the spirit of prophecy.

Clearly this testimony of Jesus is somehow connected with the spirit of prophecy. We'll expand on that in just a moment. But notice one other detail: it is John's "brethren" that have this testimony.

That becomes significant when we consider a nearly identical verse later in the same book. Here, John again falls at the feet of the angel. But notice the subtle change in wording when the angel responds this time:

Revelation 22:8-9
And I John saw these things, and heard them. And when I had heard and seen, I fell down to worship before the feet of the angel which shewed me these things. Then saith he unto me, See thou do it not: for I am thy fellowservant, and of thy brethren the prophets, and of them which keep the sayings of this book: worship God.

Did you catch that? John's brethren are the prophets. And those brethren, we read earlier, are the ones who have the testimony of Jesus. In other words, the remnant doesn't just have a decent understanding of prophecy. No, the spirit of prophecy is something only prophets have. The remnant must have a prophet.

Now if you are familiar with Seventh-day Adventists, you know we claim to have this identifying mark as well. We believe Ellen White was given the prophetic gift, and fulfilled the role of prophet in the early days of our church. And we often refer to her work as the testimony of Jesus, or the Spirit of prophecy. But I'd like to suggest, there's actually much more to the story.

But first a couple obvious questions...

Really, a Prophet?

Historically, prophets have been pretty scarce through the last 2000 years of Christian history. So scarce in fact, some have concluded the prophetic gift ended with the death of Jesus. But is that true?

Actually, the book of Acts records several New Testament prophets. Judas and Silas are both identified as prophets (Acts 15:32). A number of prophets resided at Antioch (Acts 13:1). Paul encountered a prophet named Agabus when he was in Caesarea (Acts 21:10). And Philip the Evangelist, had four daughters which prophesied (Acts 21:8-9). Clearly, this gift was present in the early church.

Furthermore, prophecy is the only gift mentioned in all three lists of spiritual gifts promised to the church (Romans 12:6, I Corinthians 12:10, Ephesians 4:11). And God states specifically that these gifts were to continue "till we all come in the unity of the faith" (Ephesians 4:12).

But why then such a scarcity of prophets through so much of the history of the Christian church? What caused the prophetic gift to be withdrawn?

Here's the explanation: in times of apostasy, God often withdraws the prophetic gift. When certain Jews came to Ezekiel for a message from the Lord, God answered: "As I live, saith the Lord God, I will not be inquired of by you" (Ezekiel 20:3). Why? "Because they had not executed my judgments, but had despised my statutes, and had polluted my sabbaths" (Ezekiel 20:24). In the same way, When King Saul turned away from God, he soon discovered "God is departed from me, and answereth me no more, neither by prophets, nor by dreams" (I Samuel 28:15).

It makes sense then, that during the dark centuries of papal apostasy, the prophetic voice would go silent. And then later, as God's people took steps to restore the Law of God, and the Sabbath in particular, to its proper place, that the prophetic gift might be restored.

Why Now?

In fact, there's a really good reason to expect a prophet in more recent times. And it's that God tends to organize his prophets into teams. That is, He gives one prophet an important message, involving time. And then He sends another prophet at the end of that time period to announce its completion. Consider:

- God prophesied through Abraham that Israel would go into Egypt for 400 years. Then he raised up Moses at the end of that time period to announce it was time to leave.

- God prophesied through Jeremiah there would be 70 years of Babylonian captivity. Then he raised up the prophet Zechariah to announce that time period had come to an end.

- God prophesied through Daniel that the Messiah would arrive at the end of 69 weeks of years. Then He raised up John the Baptist to announce its fulfillment.

In a similar way, God prophesied through Daniel the birth of His endtime movement in 1844. Should it surprise us then that God would raise up a prophet at the termination of that prophecy, to make sure we didn't miss it?

Lacking No Gift

The real purpose for this gift, however, goes back to our original question: how could a movement arise with so much insight to the Scriptures?

It took the prophetic gift.

You see, the real "spirit" of prophecy is the Holy Spirit. The prophets of old could only testify about things to come because they had the "Spirit of Christ" in them (I Peter 1:10-11). These prophets "spake as they were moved by the Holy Ghost" (II Peter 1:21). In this sense, then, the message of a prophet is indeed the "testimony of Jesus".

Earth's final movement could arise because it had Jesus speaking directly to it.

Here's another way to think about it. The testimony of Jesus is His statement, or witness, that He would send the Holy Spirit after His departure. And that this Spirit would show them things to come. Clearly, Jesus made those promises before ascending to heaven:

John 14:26
But the Comforter, which is the Holy Ghost, whom the Father will send in my name, he shall teach you all things, and bring all things to your remembrance, whatsoever I have said unto you.

John 16:13
Howbeit when he, the Spirit of truth, is come, he will guide you into all truth: for he shall not speak of himself; but whatsoever he shall hear, that shall he speak: and he will shew you things to come.

The book of Ephesians tells us Jesus was faithful to fulfill this promise: "when he ascended up on high, he led captivity captive, and gave gifts unto men" (Ephesians 4:8). And the gifts He sent included prophets: "And he gave some, apostles; and some, prophets; and some, evangelists; and some, pastors and teachers" (Ephesians 4:11).

In other words, Jesus testified that he would send the Holy Spirit. And that the Holy Spirit would give gifts to men. Having a prophet is one of those gifts.

Of course, to have the testimony of Jesus fully confirmed, the church would need to have all the gifts. Follow carefully:

> *I Corinthians 1:4-8*
> *I thank my God always on your behalf, for the grace of God which is given you by Jesus Christ; That in every thing ye are enriched by him, in all utterance, and in all knowledge; Even as the testimony of Christ was confirmed in you: So that ye come behind in no gift; waiting for the coming of our Lord Jesus Christ: Who shall also confirm you unto the end, that ye may be blameless in the day of our Lord Jesus Christ.*

Here Paul is thanking God for the grace given to the church in Corinth. That they were blessed as a church in all utterance and knowledge. And that the "testimony of Christ" was "confirmed" in them. What did that confirmation mean? Basically, that they came behind "in no gift". That all the gifts of the Spirit, including the gift of prophecy, were present.

In other words, what we see in Revelation, is that God's endtime movement will experience having the testimony of Christ confirmed in them once again. That no gift will be lacking—including the incredible gift of having a prophet. In fact, Paul hinted at this in his letter to Corinth, that it would be especially true of the church "waiting for the coming of our Lord Jesus Christ".

Why? Because only the full complement of gifts can "confirm you unto the end" and make us "blameless in the day of our Lord Jesus Christ" (I Corinthians 1:8). In other words, it took all the gifts, and especially the gift of prophecy, to raise up the final movement. And we must continue to value these gifts, if we dare hope to finish the work we've been given.

Prophecy is just one gift, but it's an important one. And the Seventh-day Adventist church could never have risen with it. It's a critical explanation to our question about how the movement came about.

And the fact this gift reappeared right on time is just one more proof, we've found the right movement.

Puzzle Pieces
Chapter 6

In the last days it shall come to pass,
that the mountain of the house of the LORD
shall be established in the top of the mountains,
and it shall be exalted above the hills.
Micah 4:1

So far we've surveyed a good number of prophecies, and together, these prophecies give us all the information we need to identify the remnant. It's pretty simple actually:

Look for a movement raised up supernaturally, in such a way that it would reassess every one of its core beliefs and come out the other end of that process with a solidly biblical understanding of each point.

Look for a movement that has a clear understanding of Bible prophecy, particularly regarding the enemy's last two great powers: the Antichrist, and False Prophet. And the Mark of the Beast. Better still, find a group that teaches the everlasting gospel in its correct prophetic context.

Look for a movement able to peer through the veil, and into the sanctuary in heaven—with a thorough understanding of the priestly ministry of Christ, Old Testament typology, and the glorious promises of the new covenant.

And last...

Look for a movement, blessed with all the gifts of the Spirit, including the gift of prophecy. A group that has the testimony of Jesus confirmed in them, so that they come behind in no gifts while waiting for Christ's return.

There's only one group that matches any of these points: the Seventh-day Adventist church.

But this is hardly all the evidence. The Bible actually predicts the birth of this movement in detail. Let's look at that now.

The Little Book

You can find the story in chapter 10 of Revelation. Here John sees a mighty angel, standing with one foot on the sea, and the other on the earth. The most significant detail about this angel, is that he has a little book in his hand, apparently freshly opened.

There's only one book of the Bible that was ever closed, and that's the book of Daniel. To him, the angel said: "Go thy way, Daniel: for the words are closed up and sealed till the time of the end" (Daniel 12:9). He was also told this book would be unsealed at the end, for the next verse says "none of the wicked shall understand; but the wise shall understand" (Daniel 12:10).

Bible scholars have linked these two passages together and concluded the little book in the hand of the angel must be the book of Daniel. And they link this story historically, to those early Advent preachers who were studying the time prophecies of Daniel, and particularly, the 2300 year prophecy that concluded in 1844. It was as if the book had suddenly opened up—and they were able to grasp things, no one had ever seen before.

In what is obviously an enacted parable, a voice from heaven then instructs John to take the book and eat it: "Go and take the little book which is open in the hand of the angel ... Take it, and eat it up" (Revelation 10:8-9). He also warns him what the experience would be like: "it shall make thy belly bitter, but it shall be in thy mouth sweet as honey" (Revelation 10:9).

And again, the experience of those early Advent preachers, is a perfect match. Their belief Jesus would come in 1844 filled their heart with inexpressible joy and excitement. To use John's words: "it was in my mouth sweet as honey". But when Jesus failed to return at the time expected, that joy turned to sorrow, in what we now call the Great Disappointment. Or to quote John again: "as soon as I had eaten it, my belly was bitter" (Revelation 10:10). The experience they passed through, matches these verses perfectly.

Immediately after, we're told what comes next: "And he said unto me, thou must prophesy again before many peoples, and nations, and tongues, and kings" (Revelation 10:11). These believers would have to pick themselves back up, get back into the Bible, figure out their mistake, and dig out another, even brighter message from heaven.

In fact, the very next verse tells us where to look for this new message: "and the angel stood, saying, Rise, and measure the temple of God" (Revelation 11:1). As we've already discussed, they turned their attention to the sanctuary in heaven at the exact time predicted, and passage after passage unlocked to their minds in quick succession. In fact, it led to all the topics we've looked at so far, falling into place.

Revelation in particular became more clear. They saw Christ clothed as a priest. They saw furniture from the temple such as the seven branched candlestick and the altar of incense. They saw Jesus move into the Most Holy Place, when they read how the temple of God "opened in heaven" to a room with "the ark of his testament". They realized the temple was heaven's nerve center, with angels coming and going, delivering important messages from the throne. And they noticed in the New Jerusalem, that there was "no temple therein", for the sin problem had finally been resolved.

The sanctuary proved a powerful tool for unlocking much of Revelation.

The Heart of Revelation

In fact, when you view Revelation through the lens of the sanctuary you notice something quite interesting. First, it clearly seems to be divided into three main sections.

The seven churches, seals, and trumpets described in the first 9 chapters, are all introduced by scenes that were staged in the Holy place. Given that Jesus began his ministry in this apartment soon after ascending to heaven, these prophecies appear to cover the whole history of the church from the beginning of the Christian epoch on down. And indeed, Bible scholars interpret these chapters as largely being a part of our past.

In chapter 15, we see the temple fill with smoke—and no one is able to enter. This kicks off a series of events typically understood to still be in the future: the close of probation, the plagues, the second coming, the millenium, the New Jerusalem, etc. These last 7 chapters are part of what is to come.

That leaves chapters 10-14 for our day. And indeed, these chapters are filled with language appropriate for the anti-typical day of atonement. Eat the little book. Go measure the temple. The ark was seen. The hour of his judgment is come. Understanding the sanctuary enables us to discern these middle 5 chapters are the critical ones for our day right now.

And what do these chapters communicate? They describe the experience of the early Advent preachers who discovered the prophecy in Daniel of the 2300 days, and their great disappointment in 1844. And their call to prophecy again, and in particular—to preach a message about the temple. The prophecy of the two witnesses in chapter 11, represents an important endtime resurgence of the Old and New Testaments. A shift back to a fuller understanding of the Bible. A restitution of all those truths spoken by the mouth of his prophets. We then see the history of the true church in the next chapter, culminating in the final remnant. It tells us where it would rise, and when, that it keeps the commandments, and that it has the testimony of Jesus--a prophet in its midst. In the next chapter, we find the enemies of this movement, the Antichrist and False Prophet, and the final crisis this movement was raised up to warn the world about. And then in the last of those chapters, there's the three angels messages that give the exact message of this movement--the everlasting gospel in its proper prophetic context.

To put it just a bit differently, the sanctuary helps us understand something critical about Revelation. That the 5 chapters most relevant to our day, are filled with information about one specific thing: the identity of the movement.

Their experience. Their characteristics. Their message. Their work. We know when, where, why, and how. Everything we could possibly need to identify it.

The Second Biggest Prophecy

In many ways, it reminds me of another set of prophecies: the prophecies about the Messiah. Think about it.

We know where Jesus would be born.
We know when He would arrive
We know details about His birth.
We know what His work would involve.
We know what He would preach.
We know that He would be executed.
And we know He would rise again.

In fact we know scores of things about Him. These prophecies are scattered through many Old Testament books. They were written by different people, in different ages. But they were all given to communicate one vital truth: Jesus is the promised Messiah, the Savior of the world.

The prophecies about the movement are similar. We know when and where it would rise. The details of how it came about. We know its work and message. And many other important characteristics. And as we'll continue to study in the coming chapters of this book, we know quite a bit about its future destiny, too.

And these prophecies are scattered all through the Bible as well. Written by different people, in different ages. And we've been given this information, for one specific purpose: so we can identify, and then unite with, that movement.

By my estimation, it's the second biggest prophecy in the Bible!

There's no question about it. This information is important to God. He wants us to find the movement. Let's all determine to study this question out, and make a firm decision to follow God's prophetic instruction for our day.

Death in the Pot
Chapter 7

And it came to pass, as they were eating of the pottage,
that they cried out, and said,
O thou man of God, there is death in the pot.
II Kings 4:40

God has given us all the information we need to identify God's final movement as the Seventh-day Adventist church. It has all the identifying marks, and it lines up with them perfectly. There can be no mistake about it.

But through the years, I've seen numerous individuals chase after one tangent or another, get confused, then side-tracked, only to leave the church at last. Somehow, they become convinced God is raising up some other movement. That God has abandoned His church, and moved on somewhere else. That if we had only accepted their particular favorite theological tweak, we could have finally gotten things right as a church.

Prophetically, this view is problematic. First, there's zero indication in Scripture that God plans to bring some remnant out of the remnant. And second, if He were to do that, the new group could never match all the identifying marks. After all, the

Seventh-day Adventist church is locked in time. Only its founders went through the experience of 1844. They were the ones God gathered from every denomination to establish the theological and prophetic base we enjoy today. That's the church with the founding prophet. Groups can splinter off, but our rich historical development can never be repeated.

Today, I want to share a thought or two about how to avoid being led astray. How to avoid falling for one of the many deceptions floating around out there and not be shaken out of the movement.

It has to do with the story of Elisha and the Gourds

Elisha and the Gourds

Elisha is actually one of my favorite Old Testament characters—thanks to all those crazy miracles:

Healing Naaman of leprosy
Raising the little boy who died, only to start sneezing
Helping a widow get out of debt by filling pots with oil
The floating axehead
The vision of the chariots of fire
The bears and those disrespectful youth
Blinding the Syrian armies

And even after he died—the most astonishing story of them all: some men are coming along to bury a friend and they run into a band of Moabites. They duck into a cave to hide and set down the body they are carrying. It happens to be Elisha's sepulcher, and when the dead body touches his old bones, their friend suddenly springs back to life and jumps to his feet. Wow, what a story!

Well the tale of the toxic gourds is another one of those miracles. Here is what happened:

II Kings 4:38-40
And Elisha came again to Gilgal: and there was
a dearth in the land; and the sons of the prophets
were sitting before him: and he said unto his
servant, Set on the great pot, and seethe pottage
for the sons of the prophets. And one went out into
the field to gather herbs, and found a wild vine,
and gathered thereof wild gourds his lap full, and
came and shred them into the pot of pottage: for
they knew them not. So they poured out for the
men to eat. And it came to pass, as they were
eating of the pottage, that they cried out, and
said, O thou man of God, there is death in the pot.
And they could not eat thereof.

It's not just a dramatic story, however. It's an enacted parable. Like many of Elisha's miracles, there are vital lessons here. In particular, it outlines the development of what I call "death in the pot" syndrome. Notice the steps:

1. It starts with a dearth, or famine. When people are hungry.

We get that way sometimes don't we? Maybe the pastor is not feeding us as well as we think he ought. We get a little bored with the knowledge we have. A desire awakens for something original, something exciting. We start looking around for some flashy new insight, in hopes of bringing a little zest into our stale experience. Like the children of Israel eating their manna, we're not satisfied. Not content.

This tendency is dangerous however, because it can lead to serious problems. Which is why the Bible gives so many warnings about focusing our study on fringe subjects:

Repeatedly, Paul warns us to avoid speculative and controversial topics. "But foolish and unlearned questions avoid, knowing that they do gender strifes" (II Timothy 2:23). Avoid "profane and vain babblings" (I Timothy 6:20). Don't focus on "questions and strifes of words, whereof cometh envy, strife, railings, evil surmisings, perverse disputings... from such withdraw thyself" (I Timothy 6:4-5). "Neither give heed to fables and endless genealogies, which minister questions, rather than godly edifying" (I Timothy 1:4).

That last point is actually quite significant. If you don't feel you are being fed spiritually, don't focus on seeking out new insights and discoveries—which can be dangerous distractions. Rather, focus more on the personal implementation of the truths you do have. "Exercise thyself rather unto godliness" (I Timothy 4:7). Focus on "wholesome words, even the words of our Lord Jesus Christ, and to the doctrine which is according to godliness" (I Timothy 6:3). That will bring all the challenge you ever need to keep your walk with God a daring adventure.

2. Next, someone goes out and starts looking around.

Most of the people were ok with the situation. They may not have had a lot of food, but there was enough to make some soup. And if you notice a little later in the story (vs 42), God had already arranged for someone to bring more food. The next meal was on its way!

But one guy was not content with what God had provided. He began thinking he might be able to add something to the meal. That if he looked around, he might be able to find something "out there". And find something, he did: a wild vine, with toxic gourds growing on it.

The Bible frequently uses the vine as a symbol for the church—but it's always a cultivated, well tended vine. This was a wild one, outside God's final movement. That's what made it so dangerous.

If you don't want death in your pot, be careful about going outside God's church for spiritual food. Stick to recognized, and respected teachers.

The Bible warns us of this danger as well. It says to "try the spirits" because "many false prophets are gone out into the world" (I John 4:1). Paul warns us to "beware lest any man spoil you through philosophy and vain deceit" (Colossians 2:8). And again, "let no man beguile you of your reward" with their speculations about "things which he hath not seen" (Colossians 2:18). It has happened to countless others, and it is foolish to think we are beyond the possibility of deception. "Beware lest ye also, being led away with the error of the wicked, fall from your own stedfastness" (II Peter 3:17).

The fact is, God has given us "first apostles, secondarily prophets, thirdly teachers" and set them "in the church" (I Corinthians 12:28). Their work is to help bring about "the unity of the faith" (Ephesians 4:13). False teachers do the opposite. They speak "perverse things, to draw away disciples after them" (Acts 20:30).

Actually, that's a simple way to tell if you've found toxic gourds: If the teachings lead you away from God's organized church—they are trouble. Don't eat them!

3. Next, the man loads up with gourds.

Here's what I've noticed: when someone stumbles on to one of these wild vines, they tend to start filling up in secret. Rather than telling someone what they are doing, they go deeper and deeper, privately. Usually, no one knows anything has happened until they are fully loaded!

The problem with filling up on gourds, is that it opens a person to the spell of the enemy. They become so entranced, supernaturally, it becomes extraordinarily difficult to reason with them. So captivated, it becomes virtually impossible to escape.

The Bible describes this process as well. By "intruding into those things which he hath not seen" they become "vainly puffed up by his fleshly mind" (Colossians 2:18). They fall into "the snare of the devil" and "are taken captive by him at his will" (II Timothy 2:26). They become "entangled" again, are brought into "bondage", and "overcome" (II Peter 2:18-20). They "wax worse and worse, deceiving, and being deceived" (II Timothy 3:13). Ultimately, the Bible warns they will "utterly perish in their own corruption" (II Peter 2:12).

Don't underestimate the power of these gourds. It's supernatural. Satanic. Secretly gathering them up, puts you on the enemy's enchanted ground. Don't do it.

4. Next, the gourd gets shredded and mixed into the soup

Once a person is loaded up with wild gourds, it starts coming out in various ways. It starts mixing itself into how they think. It starts leaking out in little things they say. And that's what happens here. Our guy starts cutting the gourds into tiny pieces and mixing them in with the rest of the soup.

It's the age old mingling of truth and error. Which is what makes deception so subtle. So much of it sounds right. We don't always catch the little errors or mistakes at first. Be cautious when you hear someone introduce new ideas with: "I didn't agree with everything, but there's some good stuff in there". Chances are good, they didn't filter out everything either...

Just because a person uses a lot of Scripture or inspired quotations, does not prove his position is correct. It could actually be an indication there's a problem. After all, most Bible truths can be explained very simply, in just a verse or two.

Here's how the Bible describes such teachers: "their mouth speaketh great swelling words" (Jude 1:16). We are to beware "lest any man should beguile you with enticing words" (Colossians 2:4). To be on guard that "no man deceive you with vain words" (Ephesians 5:6). We are instructed to "mark them which cause divisions and offences contrary to the doctrine which ye have learned" because they "deceive the hearts of the simple" by "good words and fair speeches" (Romans 16:17-18). It happens all the time.

Watch out when someone tries to overwhelm you with more information than you can process. It's nearly impossible to sort everything out when it's all mixed together in the pot. You can't help but miss some of the tiny bits of error, and will end up swallowing at least a few along with the truth.

5) The final step? They start giving the soup to others.

It's pretty much inevitable. Give most people a little time, and they will start promoting their secret views eventually. Pushing them on others.

Often it's done quietly, subtly, with a focus on new members, who are naive and inexperienced. Or disaffected members, who are negative and critical. And sometimes it can spread widely, before you realize what is happening. One day you wake up and notice there's not only death in the pot—but half the church has been eating it!

Sometimes, it becomes so problematic, the church must resort to discipline—and someone gets disfellowshipped. If enough people are infected, the whole church may need to be disbanded. It happens.

Titus 3:10-11
A man that is an heretick [Greek: divisive] after the first and second admonition reject; knowing that he that is such is subverted, and sinneth, being condemned of himself.

They can't really help themselves. They will "arise, speaking perverse things, to draw away disciples after them" (Acts 20:30). "There shall be false teachers among you, who privily shall bring in damnable heresies... And many shall follow their pernicious ways" (II Peter 2:1-2). "For there are many unruly and vain talkers and deceivers... who subvert whole houses, teaching things which they ought not" (Titus 1:10-11).

If these individuals were to focus on reaching out to the world, and bringing people to Christ, they would be less problematic. But their tendency is to focus their attention on proselytizing those already within the church. Like parasites, their focus is the host body. When you encounter an individual trying to convert church members to their peculiar ideas, and contrary to the established teachings of the body, you know you have trouble. The church has to confront it.

Our Only Safety

There's plenty of danger around, all right. Lots of wild vines and lots of wild gourds. And lots of people putting these gourds into lots of pots. And worst of all, lots of people eating it up!

But you can avoid it all if you:

1) Don't tolerate an appetite for chasing new light
2) Stay close to respected remnant teachers
3) Don't fill up in secret on something new you find
4) Avoid trying to digest truth and error together, and
5) Just say no when someone offers strange soup!

The guy in our story was naive. The Bible says he didn't know the gourds were poisonous. But that doesn't mean he was completely innocent.

No one told him to go out looking for gourds. And no one told him to gather some up. He didn't show his gourds to anyone when he got back. And he certainly didn't ask permission to add them to the pot.

Rather, he acted on his own, independently. That's the real issue, isn't it?

As pointed out earlier, God has appointed leaders in the church to shepherd and protect the flock. And their job is "the edifying of the body of Christ ... that we henceforth be no more children, tossed to an fro, and carried about with every wind of doctrine, by the sleight of men, and cunning craftiness, whereby they lie in wait to deceive" (Ephesians 4:12-14). And it's through their ministry that "the whole body" is "fitly joined together" (Ephesians 4:16). We need them!

Which is how Ellen White describes our only safe path:

The only safety for any of us is in receiving no new doctrine, no new interpretation of the Scriptures, without first submitting it to brethren of experience. Lay it before them in a humble, teachable spirit, with earnest prayer; and if they see no light in it, yield to their judgment; for "in

the multitude of counselors there is safety."
Testimonies, vol 5, p 292.

Fortunately, this is where our tale of the toxic gourds ends up. When someone finally realized what had happened, they turned to Elisha, heaven's ordained leadership, and asked for help: "There's toxic gourds in here! What do we do?"

Elisha's answer was to add more flour to the pot. See II Kings 4:40-41. It was probably the kind you use to make bread. And that flour counteracted the poison. There was no more "harm in the pot". All their lives were spared.

God still has leaders today to help us when we get stuck in these kinds of situations. To put more bread in the pot. To throw in more truth, and help counteract the error. If you ever find yourself enchanted by some wild gourd, grab a church leader and get some help. And the quicker the better! Every moment you delay increases your risk of disaster.

Bottom line: there is only one endtime movement. God has clearly identified it, and it is locked in time. Locked in history. Don't let anyone shake you out.

Chaos Theory
Chapter 8

Let all things be done decently and in order.
I Corinthians 14:40

One of the many degrees I tinkered with for awhile in college was mathematics. And I got into some pretty weird stuff. One field of mathematics that particularly interested me at the time was chaos theory.

Essentially, chaos theory tries to analyze really complex systems to see if there is in fact some underlying pattern. It tries to see order in disorder. Or to put it differently, it looks for beauty in chaos.

Unfortunately you encounter something similar in the Seventh-day Adventist church, at times. People who aren't too sure about church organization. Who are opposed to structure in God's work. They too, seem to think there is beauty in chaos.

They may claim to hold the same doctrines as other Adventists, at least on other points, but when it comes to being part of a denomination—they aren't convinced. They are not concerned about church membership. They're reluctant to serve in church office. They typically don't support the church with their tithes. And they tend to undermine church leadership.

Some don't bother with church attendance at all.

Bottom line, they don't really believe God has raised up a movement!

Chaos theory seems to be rooted in the belief there was no organization in the early church. And that the more disorganized we become, the closer we will get to the New Testament ideal. But the reality is, the early church began building structure almost immediately.

Today I want to explore this topic more fully.

Assembling Together

Let's start with something pretty basic. The Bible is definite about the importance of being plugged into a local church. Paul made that clear explicitly, in the book of Hebrews:

> *Hebrews 10:24-25*
> *And let us consider one another to provoke unto love and to good works: Not forsaking the assembling of ourselves together, as the manner of some is; but exhorting one another: and so much the more, as ye see the day approaching.*

Apparently, the bad habit of skipping church started back in Paul's day. But his admonition against that habit has lost none of its authority. In fact, it seems it is only going to become even more important, the closer we get to the end.

The Bible is actually full of these "one another" commands. Believers are to love one another, exhort one another, comfort one another, forgive one another, prefer one another, edify one another, receive one another, pray for one another, admonish one another, salute one another, serve one another, and more. If we are serious about wanting to fulfill all these commands, it makes sense we would want to spend time with "one another"!

Corporate worship is actually important. You'll find more than 100 references to "congregation" in the Bible. And even more to God's people "assembling" together. Here's just a couple:

> *Psalms 107:32*
> *Let them exalt him also in the congregation of the people, and praise him in the assembly of the elders.*

> *Psalms 111:1*
> *Praise ye the LORD. I will praise the LORD with my whole heart, in the assembly of the upright, and in the congregation.*

It's hard to imagine anyone concluding from the Bible that corporate worship is not important.

Actually, that was, and still is, the purpose of the Sabbath. Many people think the Sabbath was made holy so we could rest. I think we have it backwards. God commanded us to rest from secular work on that day so we could reserve that time for holy purposes. And particularly for worship:

> *Leviticus 23:3*
> *Six days shall work be done: but the seventh day is the sabbath of rest, an holy convocation.*

That's what the word "convocation" means. It's a gathering. A congregation of believers. An assembly for worship. And it's supposed to happen very week. If you're not using the Sabbath for this purpose, you're missing the point.

It was certainly the "custom" of Jesus to go "into the synagogue on the sabbath day" (Luke 4:16). And it was Paul's "manner" too, to go into the synagogue on the "sabbath" (Acts 17:2). And there's no question about what we will do in "the new heavens and the new earth": "from one sabbath to another, shall all flesh come to worship before me, saith the LORD" (Isaiah 66:22-23). If God's plan is for His "congregation" to "assemble" each Sabbath day throughout all eternity, shouldn't we start getting used to that here and now?

Church Leadership

It's also quite clear God designed the church to have leadership structures. In fact, the very first thing the church did was fill the vacant seat of an apostle (Acts 1:26). And one of the first things they did once the church began growing, was to appoint deacons (Acts 6:3). But the New Testament is actually full of references to specific church leaders: not just elders and deacons, but ministers, teachers, bishops, apostles, evangelists, and prophets, and so on.

There are even hints of roles for women as well. Phoebe was given the title of "servant of the church which is at Cenchrea" (Romans 16:1). The word "servant" here, is the Greek word for "deaconess". And older women with certain qualifications could be accepted into a special office for widows (I Timothy 5:9-10). Regardless, it is clear the church began creating new offices quickly as various needs arose.

And policies quickly developed related to these offices. Take the office of elder, for example. Paul spelled out the requirements for this office (I Timothy 3:1-4). And he gave instructions about how to select elders. Timothy was to "lay hands suddenly on no man" (I Timothy 5:22). Rather, they should fill a lower office first for a while and prove themselves, (I Timothy 3:13) until they were no longer "a novice" (I Timothy

3:6). They were to be set apart for their work by an official ceremony, the "laying on of the hands" (I Timothy 4:14). And there were rules about how they were to be treated: they were to be "counted worthy of double honour" (I Timothy 5:17). And "against an elder", Timothy was not to receive "an accusation, but before two or three witnesses" (I Timothy 5:19). The whole church was to recognize and respect these leaders.

My point is this, the church not only created offices, but it created structure to support those offices.

Church Membership

One responsibility of these leaders was to manage church membership. Actually, Jesus taught this principle, when he said a brother who commits a trespass, "if he neglect to hear the church, let him be unto thee as an heathen man and a publican" (Matthew 18:15-17). Furthermore, He emphasized the seriousness of this action in the very next verse: "verily I say unto you, whatsoever ye shall bind on earth shall be bound in heaven" (Matthew 18:18).

The rest of the New Testament expands on this, by providing appropriate guidelines. Paul called for disfellowshipping a member who engaged in sexual immorality (I Corinthians 5:1-5). For those who "cause divisions and offenses" contrary to established "doctrine" (Romans 16:17). For "every brother who walks disorderly" (II Thessalonians 3:6). And for various other lifestyle practices (I Corinthians 5:11).

In a similar way Paul endorsed various individuals in his letters, as a way to acknowledge their authenticity, and to encourage their support: Barnabas, Silas, Timothy, Titus, Epaphras, Mark, Aristarchus, Tychicus, Trophimus, Apollos, and more. Plus a number of women: Phoebe, Priscilla, Tryphena, Tryphosa, Persis, Julia, etc. This use of "letters of commendation" to confirm valid membership, was apparently a common practice in the early church (II Corinthians 3:1).

Managing church membership is an extremely delicate and sensitive work, and should only be done with the greatest care and tact. But it still needs to be done.

Fundamental Beliefs

The leadership of the church also played a role in determining what basic beliefs were to be considered the shared faith of the church. The primary example of this, of course, is Acts 15, when "certain men which came down from Judaea taught the brethren, and said, except ye be circumcised after the manner of Moses, ye cannot be saved" (Acts 15:1). Paul and Barnabas argued against this with "no small dissension and disputation", so the church decided to send those two to Jerusalem to settle the question with the apostles and elders there.

To make a long story short, that very first "general conference session" met and sided unanimously with Paul and Barnabas. They also "wrote letters" and sent those back along with two official representatives (Judas and Silas). This decision brought great "consolation" to the early church (Acts 15:31). And as these letters eventually spread "through the cities", "so were the churches established in the faith" (Acts 16:4-5). The church together, not individuals, settled doctrinal disputes.

The flip side to this is also true. That is, Paul was quick to share when something was his opinion, and not the official position of the church. "I speak this by permission, and not of commandment" (I Corinthians 7:6). "To the rest speak I, not the Lord" (I Corinthians 7:11). And if someone objected to one of his opinions, the church was to respond "we have no such custom, either the churches of God" (I Corinthians 11:16). In those situations, his counsel was to "let every man be fully persuaded in his own mind" (Romans 14:5).

In other words, it is the job of the church to decide what theological positions are essential for church membership, and which topics allow for some freedom of interpretation. No individual has the right to establish his own test of fellowship. Nor should any member undermine or minimize the established teachings of the church.

If a person disagrees with some core point, they can humbly seek a hearing with church leaders, and make their case. But they should always be careful to recognize and respect well-established teachings. To do otherwise, is to reveal a deeper spiritual problem. See Titus 3:9-11.

Systematic Benevolence

Of course, the real test of loyalty to a movement, is whether or not you support it financially. Or to quote a more modern cliche, we should put our money where our mouth is.

Jesus made a similar point in the sermon on the mount. By giving to God's cause, you "lay up for yourselves treasures in heaven" (Matthew 6:20). And that's important, "for where your treasure is, there will your heart be also" (Matthew 6:21). Notice it doesn't say you put your treasure where your heart is. Rather, it says wherever you put your treasure, your heart will follow.

Some argue for diverting the tithe away from the "storehouse" and for giving it to other ministries instead. I have a strong practical argument for not doing so: The moment you withdraw your support from God's church, your heart begins to withdraw as well. And your witness becomes marred. After all, how you can enthusiastically bring someone into a church you can't personally support?

It happens every time. Loyalty weakens. Involvement fades. You become negative and critical. Not to mention that withdrawing support is the quickest path to losing your ability to be a voice for positive change. Don't do it. If you want to stay plugged in spiritually, make sure you are plugged in financially.

Here's how Ellen White responded to a brother in her day on this question of the tithe:

> *I understand that you are also proclaiming that we should not pay tithe. My brother, take off thy shoes from off thy feet; for the place whereon you are standing is holy ground. The Lord has spoken in regard to paying tithes. He has said, Bring ye all the tithes into the storehouse, that there may be meat in Mine house, and prove Me now herewith, saith the Lord of hosts, if I will not open you the windows of heaven, and pour you out a blessing, that there shall not be room enough to receive it. But while He pronounces a blessing upon those who bring in their tithes, He pronounces a curse upon those who withhold them. Very recently I have had direct light from the Lord upon this question, that many Seventh-day Adventists were robbing God in tithes and offerings, and it was plainly revealed to me that Malachi has stated the case as it really is. Then how dare any man even think in his heart that a suggestion to withhold tithes and offerings is from the Lord? TM, p. 60*

I tend to look at this question more on the positive side. That our system of systematic benevolence is actually a blessing and privilege. Because I know the tithe dollars I give, are dedicated to a specific use, the support of ministers and church officers, I know my dollars are a direct investment in the global spread of God's endtime movement.

And in fact, that's what makes our church so incredibly powerful. Rather than just focusing on our own local congregation, like so many other denominations, every member is giving to a global work. Those funds are circulated and distributed all around the world where they are needed most, by leaders right on the scene in virtually every country. It's truly a global system, and it enables us to do evangelism on a massive scale.

It's what made us a worldwide movement. And it's the envy of all other churches.

If we truly believe God has raised up this movement, we should be excited about supporting it. Yes, it may be imperfect—but strangling the movement won't help. Rather, our giving helps advance the exact thing God is trying to do right now in this world: raise up a movement to finish the work.

Conclusion

Church organization has given the church countless benefits. An educational system second to none. A vast health care system. A highly respected global relief organization. A vast foreign missions network. In all these areas and more, the Seventh-day Adventist church leads the protestant world.

And the secret to it all, has been our organization:

> *As our numbers increased, it was evident that without some form of organization there would be great confusion, and the work would not be carried forward successfully ... We sought the Lord with earnest prayer that we might understand His will, and light was given by His Spirit that there must be order and thorough discipline in the church—that organization was essential. System and order are manifest in all the*

works of God throughout the universe. Order is the law of heaven, and it should be the law of God's people on the earth. We had a hard struggle in establishing organization. Notwithstanding that the Lord gave testimony after testimony upon this point, the opposition was strong and it had to be met again and again. But we knew that the Lord God of Israel was leading us, and guiding by His providence. We engaged in the work of organization, and marked prosperity attended this advance movement. TM, p 26-27.

Chaos theory may have a place in mathematics. But it has no place anywhere in the church. God wants "all things" to be done "decently and in order" (I Corinthians 14:40). Even more so, when it comes to His endtime movement.

Without organization, there would only be, well, chaos.

Finishing the Work
Chapter 9

Jesus saith unto them,
My meat is to do the will of him that sent me,
and to finish his work.
John 4:34

I still remember one of my very first speaking trips. Since then, I've flown more times than I care to count. But at the time it was a big deal: I was a young preacher no one had ever heard of, and I had been invited to fly from California to New York, to do a week long series of meetings. Exciting!

At one of the meetings, I noticed a tall, dignified looking gentleman come in, wearing a pin-stripe suit and sharp felt hat, that made him look like something out of a gangster movie. And I caught him watching me pretty intensely.

Afterward he came up, and said he wanted to talk about something, and asked if we could meet. I told him I was free during the day, and he offered to send his chauffeur down the next morning to pick me up.

That next morning, I found myself walking into his office building and being escorted up to the top floor where he had his office. I sat down, and he began to tell me his story.

This man believed he had been given a gift for making money. As a young man he had started a company that had done extremely well. He cashed out for millions, invested it, and lost everything. He started another company and it had taken off too. He cashed out, reinvested, and lost it all again. Now he was working on his third company and it was prospering too.

Somewhere along the way he had come to the conclusion, that his previous financial losses were the result of him not dedicating his abilities to God. That he needed to consecrate his business skills and apply them to the Lord's work. He didn't want to make the same mistake a third time, so he was developing a ministry plan, and wanted to know my thoughts.

It was all sketched out on a giant corporate organizational chart. There were various for-profit business entities used to fund a wide range of interlocking ministry components. Some pieces I could recognize: health work, publishing, missions. But with my limited business background, it was mostly a confusing maze. I wasn't quite sure what to say.

Then a little box down in the corner of the chart caught my eye. It was labeled "finishing the work". I pointed to it and asked what it represented. I'll never forget his answer. Looking me straight in the eyes, he said "we believe there is still a missing key to finishing the work, and we're leaving room in our plans for when God reveals it."

I've thought about that encounter many times since. Is there indeed some missing key? And if so, what is it? What will it really take to finish the work...

The Missing Key

I'm sure there's not just one key. A lot of things have to come together for the work to be finished. But sometimes it feels like we are tantalizingly close. That somewhere, we've just missed some small thing. And that if we could just figure out what that one thing was, the work could explode dramatically. That we're sitting on a rocket engine, and we only need to enter one last code to start the ignition sequence.

Yes, I really do think we live in exciting times!

Let me tell you what I think that missing key is. For nearly 30 years, virtually my entire adult life, I've pursued a single vision with single-minded focus: to try and jumpstart a process that leads to spiritual multiplication. Looking back, I'm sometimes surprised at how little I've wavered from that vision. It's still the driving force behind everything I do.

As I mentioned in the last chapter, I was pretty good with numbers when I first became a Christian, and I knew the difference between an arithmetic series and an exponential sequence. The first plods along at a steady, consistent pace. The other starts slow, but accelerates, and quickly becomes explosive.

The difference between winning 100 members to Christ each year (Plan A) and winning just 1 person a year, but also training him to reproduce each and every year (Plan B) illustrates the point. Consider the preliminary results of these two plans in the table below:

Year	Plan A	Plan B
1	100	2
2	200	4
3	300	8
4	400	16
5	500	32
6	600	64
7	700	128
8	800	256
9	900	512
10	1000	1024

The results seem comparable for the first 10 years. But Plan A merely produces 1000 converts. Spiritual babes, unlikely to ever reproduce. Many will be gone within months. In contrast, Plan B produces 1000+ reproducing workers, all thoroughly trained, one at a time. But the results diverge even more dramatically over the next 10 years:

Year	Plan A	Plan B
11	1100	2,048
12	1200	4,096
13	1300	8,192
14	1400	16,384
15	1500	32,768
16	1600	65,536
17	1700	131,072
18	1800	262,144
19	1900	524,288
20	2000	1,048,576

During these next ten years, Plan A produces another 1000 converts. But Plan B explodes, because those first 1000 workers have now all multiplied and become another 1000 each! All still done at the same steady pace–one person at a time. It reminds me of this promise in Isaiah:

Isaiah 60:22
A little one shall become a thousand, and a small
one a strong nation: I the LORD will hasten it in
his time.

I believe that verse captures God's plan for every believer. That the "each one reach one" idea is doable. That God's promises are ours for the taking!

I'll spare you the numbers were this to continue another 10 years, but here's the nutshell version: Plan A continues to get its normal results, netting another 1000 baptisms or so. But Plan B is now producing 1000's of baptisms every day. New members, all equipped in time to reach out and win thousands more.

By the end of this third decade, Plan A is sitting at a total of around 3000 believers. But Plan B is within spitting distance of reaching the entire world. It's produced over a billion highly-skilled, well-trained workers. It's the fulfillment of another amazing promise:

> *Jeremiah 33:22*
> *As the host of heaven cannot be numbered, neither the sand of the sea measured: so will I multiply the seed of David my servant, and the Levites that minister unto me.*

Given the extraordinary contrast in the results, how could any one, serious about finishing the work, give their life to anything but spiritual multiplication?

It's Not Easy

Unfortunately, kickstarting a process of spiritual multiplication has proved harder than I anticipated. The enemy has been interfering with that process for centuries and has shackled up the vast majority of believers, so that few are consistently winning souls to Christ.

Whether it is due to poor internalization of the word, lack of prayer, sin in the life, ineffective ministry models, or any number of other causes, explosive multiplication is being blocked.

And it's a cause for concern. When we think in terms of multiplication, each broken link in the process has severe consequences. One new member who leaves the church, is not just a single person, but a loss of the 1000 believers he might have become ten years down the road if properly nurtured and trained. A person who survives church membership, but never learns to reproduce, is not much better. While we are happy that member is still around, in the grand scheme of things, a loss of 999 potential members is only marginally better than the loss of 1000 potential members.

If we could figure out what is hindering this process and get it fixed, we would be standing on the brink of an incredible, spiritual chain reaction! Thousands could quickly be mobilized all around the world, and begin multiplying exponentially. We would be astounded at how fast things could advance. The final movements would indeed be rapid ones!

Exciting thought, isn't it?

Setting Priorities

There's little doubt in my mind, that this is how the Great Commission will be finished. By actually doing the great commission—making disciples who obey all Christ's commands (Matthew 28:19-20). Including the command to go make other disciples!

And it's certainly how the New Testament church did it. "The Lord added to the church daily such as should be saved" (Acts 2:47). "And the number of the disciples multiplied in Jerusalem greatly" (Acts 6:7). And they "went everywhere preaching the word" (Acts 8:4). I won't drag out all the evidence for multiplication here, because I've written about it elsewhere many times before. But I do want to suggest, that if it is true, it implies certain priorities.

Simply put, if we really want to see multiplication break

out, we have to focus on equipping every believer to reproduce. And that means thorough training.

And I don't just mean superficial witnessing training. We need to promote and encourage the deep internalization of Scripture, until it is the true power source of every worker. We must teach the basics of personal, practical discipleship: ernest Bible study, fervent prayer, diligent time management and much more. A biblical lifestyle of discipleship is the foundation for all effective ministry. And we must get serious about teaching all aspects of evangelism, from ministry development principles, to small groups, to personal Bible studies, to public evangelism, and so on. Members must be well-equipped to reach out.

This is the three step model we've been teaching at FAST pretty much from the start: take in God's Word effectively, live it out practically, and then pass it on consistently. And it's the structure we've used to organize our entire library of training resources. Pretty much everything falls into one of three tracks: Bible memorization, personal discipleship, and ministry leadership. I'm sure our tools are far from perfect, but they are laser focused on one day achieving that goal of rapid reproduction. That goal of massive multiplication.

To get every member trained, we also need to think a bit differently about our churches. I believe we need to get serious about transforming every church into a training center. Only a handful of members will go online to seek out training. Praise God for them! But the rest will have to be reached through patient, persevering, personal effort. We should have training classes in every church. Provide opportunities for growth to every member. Give them access to tools and resources. In short, we must do everything in our power, to equip every member for service.

This will not be easy either. Most churches tend to focus more on maintaining their various systems and structures.

There's a place for that. And as a result, they tend to put their emphasis on programs, not people. But the reality is, these things will never finish the work. The need is always going to be more workers. "The harvest truly is plenteous, but the labourers are few" (Matthew 9:37). Somehow we must redirect our strategic plans to prioritize transforming churches into training centers that empower every member for service.

This has been a second area we've worked hard on at FAST. To assist church leaders in making that transformation. We offer options to put all our tools and resources in the hands of every member, along with access to experienced guides and coaches. But whatever tools you use, this point is key: to finish the work, church transformation is essential.

Bottom line: multiplication is the missing key. But multiplication won't be achieved without training. And training won't happen until our churches give multiplication the priority it deserves.

Exciting times are just ahead. People are starting to catch the vision. And they are engaging in this work of training. Lives are being changed. And souls are being won. And here and there, churches are starting to grow. There is still much to do, but it is certain to accelerate, in God's time. Like a giant snowball. And before long, faster than you think, it will become a mighty movement, indeed.

The work really is almost finished. The best days for God's people are just ahead.

Times of Refreshing
Chapter 10

Repent ye therefore, and be converted,
that your sins may be blotted out,
when the times of refreshing shall come
from the presence of the Lord.
Acts 3:19

We've covered a lot of ground in this book so far, haven't we?

The first half looked largely at the prophetic marks God has given to help us identify God's endtime movement. We explored how God would raise up a group with a clear understanding of all the Bible's basic truths. That there would be a restitution of all its core teachings, and that God would draw people from many different denominations, and organize them all into just one group.

We saw that God would have an endtime people committed to giving an endtime message to every nation, kindred, tongue, and people. Not only would it expose the identify of the Antichrist and the False Prophet, but it would warn the world about earth's final test on the mark of the beast. We also saw that the real issue in this crisis was a correct understanding of the everlasting gospel.

We examined the incredible hermeneutics of the apostle Paul, in his treatise on the order of Melchisedec. That Jesus was indeed our High Priest, ministering on our behalf, in the temple of heaven. And that God needed an endtime movement to understand the full implications of that. To understand the terms of the new covenant, so they could share the good news with the world.

We traced the path of God's true church through history, noting when and where it would arise. And what its chief characteristics were. We also noted that God would give this endtime remnant a special gift: a prophet to help confirm the fulfillment of an important time prophecy. We saw that the testimony of Christ would be confirmed in this movement, so that it came behind in no gift while waiting for the return of Christ. And how the prophetic gift especially, would be critical to the formation of the movement.

And last, we looked at the story of the "little book", and how it matched exactly the story of how this endtime movement came into existence. Beginning with the opening up of sweet truths hidden in the book of Daniel, on through a difficult, bitter disappointment, to finally the reception, and then proclamation of an exciting, and even more powerful, prophetic message.

In many ways, these prophecies resemble the prophecies of the Messiah–which are scattered all through the Bible, written by different writers in different times, yet they all point to one single fulfillment: Jesus Christ. Similarly, prophecies of the movement can be found all through Scripture. These tell when and where it would rise, its message and work, and more. And just like those messianic prophecies, there is only one possible match: the Seventh-day Adventist church.

Then we looked at two of Satan's chief strategies to shake people out of this movement. One is to entice believers with some kind of "new light", wild gourds from outside God's church that have the power to enchant and then hopelessly entangle any who gather them up. It inevitably brings contention and then division. Ultimately, it leads to separation from the church.

The other strategy is what I called "chaos theory". The idea that there is something beautiful or biblical about disorder in God's church. That God is somehow opposed to church organization. We then examined the New Testament church in detail, and saw that it created structures and systems right from the beginning. And that organization is a vital key to success in God's movement still today.

And then most recently, we looked at what I believe is the missing key to finishing the work. The need to redirect our focus toward spiritual multiplication. That every member can and must be equipped and empowered for service. That every church should be a training center for Christian workers. And that if we would make this our strategic priority, the work could be finished with astonishing speed.

I'm genuinely convinced our best days really are just ahead!

Encouraging Promises

I started this book by mentioning the book of Isaiah. How it had 66 chapters, and how its last 27 chapters were filled with words of comfort and cheer to those who are part of the final movement. That those chapters pull back the veil on God's future plans for it. I want to end this class by bringing it all full circle, and look at some of those promises.

It was actually these chapters that sparked this whole study. Do you remember that verse we looked at on day one?

Isaiah 51:16
And I have put my words in thy mouth, and I have
covered thee in the shadow of mine hand, that I
may plant the heavens, and lay the foundations of
the earth, and say unto Zion, Thou art my people.

I said then this verse suggests God has a special work for those who hide His Word in their mouth, and are willing to spend some extended time alone with God, hidden in the shadow of His hand. That work involves planting the spirit or essence of heaven in this world. And laying a foundation, solidly rooted in the core principles of Scripture. But it also suggests a third special work, to "say unto Zion, Thou art my people".

Over the preceding chapters, I've tried to do just that. To lay out the prophetic evidence. To assure you God has raised up a movement indeed. That it has a purpose. That it is here for a reason. That God has a special work for it to do.

But one thing I haven't said much about yet: What lies ahead for this movement?

That's where those last 27 chapters in Isaiah come in. They are filled with words of comfort and cheer, and they paint a bright picture for God's people, of what is still to come. These words should encourage and refresh the heart of every believer:

Here is how this section begins:

"Speak ye comfortably to Jerusalem, and cry unto her, that her warfare is accomplished, that her iniquity is pardoned" (Isaiah 40:2). Yes, she has brought difficult times upon herself by neglecting God's counsel unnecessarily, but that chastisement is definitely going to come to an end: "I have taken out of thine hand the cup of trembling, even the dregs of the cup of my fury; thou shalt no more drink it again" (Isaiah 51:22). "In a little wrath I hid my face from thee for a moment; but with everlasting kindness will I have mercy on thee, saith the LORD thy Redeemer" (Isaiah 54:7-8).

These chapters make it clear God is not going to forget this movement: "O Israel, thou shalt not be forgotten of me" (Isaiah 44:21). "Can a woman forget her sucking child...? yea, they may forget, yet will I not forget thee" (Isaiah 49:15). "The mountains shall depart, and the hills be removed; but my kindness shall not depart from thee" (Isaiah 54:10). Whatever painful experiences this movement may still have to endure, it will all work out in the end: "Whereas thou has been forsaken and hated ... I will make thee an eternal excellency, a joy of many generations" (Isaiah 60:15)

Don't let anyone tell you this movement is going to fail. God says: "I will give them an everlasting name, that shall not be cut off" (Isaiah 56:5). Whatever problems she has, can be corrected: "I have seen his ways, and will heal him" (Isaiah 57:18). And the reason for this has nothing to do with us. It is simply God's nature: He will show "great goodness toward the house of Israel ... according to his mercies, and according to the multitude of his lovingkindnesses" (Isaiah 63:7). "In his love and in his pity he redeemed them; and he bare them, and carried them all the days of old" (Isaiah 63:9).

God even promises success in our mission: "Israel shall be saved in the LORD with an everlasting salvation: ye shall not be ashamed nor confounded" (Isaiah 45:17). "I will direct their work in truth, and I will make an everlasting covenant with them" (Isaiah 61:8). "They shall not labour in vain, nor bring forth for trouble; for they are the seed of the blessed of the LORD, and their offspring with them" (Isaiah 65:23). And as I quoted yesterday, "A little one shall become a thousand, and a small one a strong nation: I the LORD will hasten it in his time" (Isaiah 60:22). It is going to happen—and I can't wait to see it. Can you?

Yes, God has a special message to His endtime people. And it's a message that needs to be given with a clear and certain sound:

Isaiah 62:11-12
11 Behold, the LORD hath proclaimed unto the end of the world, Say ye to the daughter of Zion, Behold, thy salvation cometh; behold, his reward is with him, and his work before him. 12 And they shall call them, The holy people, The redeemed of the LORD: and thou shalt be called, Sought out, A city not forsaken.

Verses like these fill me with incredible joy, and hope, and courage. We have no reason to be discouraged. We have nothing to fear for the future. We can have every confidence God is going to bless.

Times of refreshing are just ahead. God has promised to pour out His Spirit on His people, like never before. And the whole earth will be brightened with glory.

That's God's plan for the movement. And that future can be ours...

FAST Missions
Cutting-Edge Tools and Training

Ready to become a Revival Agent? FAST Missions can help! Our comprehensive training curriculum will give you the skills you need to take in God's Word effectively, live it out practically, and pass it on to others consistently.

Eager to start memorizing God's Word? Our powerful keys will transform your ability to hide Scripture in your heart.

Want to explore the secrets of "real life" discipleship? Our next level training zooms in on critical keys to growth, like Bible study, prayer, time management, and more.

Want to become a worker in the cause of Christ? Our most advanced training is designed to give you the exact ministry skills you need to see revival spread.

For more information, please visit us at:
WWW.FASTMISSIONS.COM

Study Guides

Looking for life-changing study guides to use in your small group or Bible study class? These resources have been used by thousands around the world. You could be next!

Survival Kit

Want to learn how to memorize Scripture effectively? These study guides will teach you 10 keys to memorization, all drawn straight from the Bible. Our most popular course ever!

Basic Training

Discover nuts and bolts keys to the core skills of discipleship: prayer, Bible study, time management, and more. Then learn how to share these skills with others. It is the course that launched our ministry!

Revival Keys

Now as never before, God's people need revival. And these guides can show you how to spark revival in your family, church, and community. A great revival is coming. Are you ready?

Online Classes

Want to try out some of the resources available at FAST? Here is just a small sampling of courses from among dozens of personal and small group study resources:

Crash Course
Discover Bible-based keys to effective memorization.
http://fast.st/cc

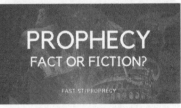

Fact or Fiction
Does the Bible really predict future events? You be the judge.
http://fast.st/prophecy

Monkey Business
Find out how evolution flunks the science test.
http://fast.st/monkey

Dry Bones
Want more of God's Spirit? Learn how to pursue revival.
http://fast.st/bones

The Lost Art
Rediscover New Testament keys to making disciples.
http://fast.st/lostart

Digital Tools

FAST offers a number of powerful "apps for the soul" you can use to grow in your walk with God. And many of these are completely free to anyone with an account. Some of these include:

Memory Engine
Our powerful review engine is designed to help ensure effective longterm Bible memorization. Give it a try, it works!

Bible Reading
An innovative Bible reading tool to help you read through the entire Bible, at your own pace, and in any order you want.

Prayer Journal
Use this tool to organize important requests, and we'll remind you to pray for them on the schedule you want.

Time Management
Learn how to be more productive, by keeping track of what you need to do and when. Just log in daily and get stuff done.

For more information about more than twenty tools like these, please visit us at *http://fast.st/tools*.

Books

If the content of this little book stirred your heart, look for these titles by the same author.

For Such A Time...
A challenging look at the importance of memorization for the last days, including topics such as the Three Angel's messages and the Latter Rain.

Moral Machinery
Discover how our spiritual, mental, and physical faculties work together using the sanctuary as a blueprint. Astonishing insights that could revolutionize your life!

The Anti-Seminary
How a broken young man stumbled his way into the secret place of the most high, and enrolled in the anti-seminary. Finding truth in all the wrong places.

Made in the USA
Middletown, DE
24 December 2021

56975693R00051